# HO HO HO!

## The Complete Book of Christmas Words

*By* Lynda Graham-Barber
*Pictures by* Betsy Lewin

*BRADBURY PRESS • NEW YORK*

*Maxwell Macmillan Canada • Toronto*
*Maxwell Macmillan International*
*New York • Oxford • Singapore • Sydney*

Bradbury Press
Macmillan Publishing Company
866 Third Avenue
New York, NY 10022

Maxwell Macmillan Canada, Inc.
1200 Eglinton Avenue East
Suite 200
Don Mills, Ontario M3C 3N1

Macmillan Publishing Company is part of the Maxwell Communication
Group of Companies.

First edition
Printed and bound in the United States of America
10   9   8   7   6   5   4   3   2   1

LIBRARY OF CONGRESS CATALOGING-IN-PUBLICATION DATA
Graham-Barber, Lynda.
    Ho Ho Ho! : the complete book of Christmas words / by Lynda
Graham-Barber ; pictures by Betsy Lewin. — 1st ed.
        p.    cm.
    Includes bibliographical references (p.      ) and index.
    Summary: Defines or explains words associated with Christmas,
including mistletoe, candle, and carol, giving their etymology and
the history of their connection with the holiday.
    ISBN 0-02-736933-1
    1. Christmas—Juvenile literature.  [1. Christmas.]  I. Lewin,
Betsy, ill.  II. Title.
GT4985.5.G72   1993
394.2′68282′014—dc20        92-6715

For Mildred Bodley Barber,
whose love and caring embody Christmas

*I heard the bells on Christmas Day*
*Their old, familiar carols play,*
*And wild and sweet*
*The words repeat*
*Of peace on earth, good-will to men!*

—Henry Wadsworth Longfellow, "Christmas Bells"

# Contents

CHRISTMAS DAY is observed
on DECEMBER 25,
in early WINTER.
A happy HOLIDAY SEASON to all!

# Christmas Day

Ho Ho Ho! The Christmas season is wrapped up in a joyful array of colors and images that dazzle our senses. Sleigh bells ring, carolers sing, trees get trimmed and stockings hung, cookies are baked, and list-reciting youngsters feel the gentle tickle of the store Santa's beard.

Christmas has become synonymous with festive decorating, gift-giving, and get-togethers. That's why it's hard to imagine our dour Puritan forefathers actually fining anyone who made a holly garland, gave someone a present, or stopped working on Christmas Day. But that's exactly what happened. To them Christmas was a sacred holiday, profaned by decorating and celebrating.

For all Christians, Christmas is a sacred day on the church calendar, celebrating the anniversary of the birth of Jesus Christ. Christmas written in Old English is *Cristes maesse*, which means "Christ's mass." Yet despite its deep religious significance, most of the customs surrounding Christmas hark back to ancient pagan rituals established long before Christianity appeared.

Chief among these pagan traditions was the Roman holiday

Saturnalia, which glorified Saturn, the god of agriculture. During this December bash, Romans decorated their houses, exchanged gifts, gambled, and feasted. In addition, the roles of slave and master were reversed, with masters waiting on slaves.

The festivities ended with a feast on December 25, *natalis solis invicti*, or "birthday of the unconquerable sun." The Romans, like many people before them, worshiped the sun. During the dark days around the winter solstice, ancient peoples worried that the sun would disappear altogether. When longer days returned, they held festivals to welcome the sun and honor nature's fertility.

On December 25, the citizens of Rome, most of whom were pagans, honored the sun-god Mithras. The cult surrounding the worship of Mithras was so accepted that by the late third century A.D., Mithraism was the state religion of the Roman Empire.

Although pagan religions like Mithraism prevailed during these early centuries, there is record of Christians in Egypt observing the birth of Christ as early as A.D. 200. Over a century later, around A.D. 350, Julius I, the bishop of Rome, officially declared December 25—the day the Romans worshiped Mithras—the anniversary of the birth of Jesus Christ. But how did a celebration that honored a pagan god come to coincide with the religious celebration of Christianity's leader?

For some two hundred years after Jesus Christ, there was little, if any, concern about when he was born. The early church placed emphasis on the day people died, the time when the soul entered heaven, not on the day they were born. In accord with this belief, saints were remembered on the anniversaries of their deaths. But the church's viewpoint about birthdays changed in the early third century.

At that time the newly established Western church found itself competing for followers with the popular pagan gods of the Romans, notably Mithras and Saturn. Most historians agree that the Christian church picked December 25 as the day to honor Jesus Christ's birth, not from actual evidence, but in an attempt to overshadow the Romans' December pagan festivals. Once the December date was set, the church forbade any feasting or merrymaking in order to disassociate Christmas from the pagan holidays.

Therefore, in its infancy Christmas was exclusively a sacred holiday. But the secular traditions refused to die, and over the years Christians began exchanging gifts and celebrating during the Christmas season, even under the disapproving eyes of church officials. The church eventually relented, and by the Middle Ages, December 25 had become the most popular holiday of the year, with religious meaning *and* secular traditions.

In England and the New England colonies, however, the Puritans forbade gift exchanges and other nonreligious practices. Because these Christmas customs had no basis in scripture, the Puritans considered them sacrilegious. As a result, the English Puritans banned all Christmas festivities in 1642. Puritans in the American colonies followed their example seventeen years later, in 1659.

During the next three centuries other settlers of America, who did not share the Puritans' austerity about Christmas, introduced their own unique holiday customs. English people in the early-seventeenth-century Virginia colonies threw elaborate balls and temporarily freed their slaves from work, a custom that probably descended from Saturnalia. In the Southwest, people of Spanish ancestry staged plays, and Scandinavians in the Midwest prepared traditional foods and left straw for the birds.

It wasn't until German immigrants came to New England in the nineteenth century that many of our conventional holiday customs began to flourish on a large scale. Across the United States today, the trappings of Christmas are unmistakable. Yet the sounds and sights of the yuletide season vary widely from one country to another. Did you ever wonder how people living in Argentina celebrate Christmas? Here's an international taste of Christmas traditions and customs as observed by people around the globe.

# Christmas Customs
# Around the World

## SWEDEN

The Christmas celebration begins on December 13, honoring
the Christian martyr Saint Lucia, who is said to bring gifts
and reveal the future. Young women wear white and carry
candles to drive away the dark, a custom that goes back to
ancient times, when December 13 was considered the
darkest day of the year. On Christmas Eve, Swedish people
celebrate Dipping Day by dipping bread into broth for good
luck, remembering a famine when only black bread and thin
broth were available. Christmas dinner includes fish and
spiced breads. People make caramels as gifts and wrap them
in brightly colored fringed papers. Children await presents
delivered by a gnome called Jultomten, who arrives in a sled
drawn by goats on Christmas Eve.

## ARGENTINA

Christmas in Argentina comes during midsummer, when the winds blow hot and dry. Holiday celebrations are usually held out-of-doors, set on tables decorated with rose blooms and jasmine. Main courses are suckling pig; rolled steak stuffed with mincemeat, olives, hard-boiled eggs, and spices; or perhaps roast peacock. Nativity scenes, which feature the manger, figures representing the holy family, and animals, are displayed in almost all homes. Children receive gifts on Three Kings Day, also known as Epiphany, January 6, in shoes set by their beds.

## SPAIN

The Christmas season begins on December 8, with the Feast of the Immaculate Conception and a ritualized dance outside Seville's cathedral. As part of the Christmas Eve celebration, huge wood or papier-mâché puppets, animated by a hidden person, dance in the streets. After midnight mass, everyone eats a huge Christmas feast, usually consisting of almond-and-milk soup; roast lamb, pork, or chicken; baked red cabbage; and sweet potato or pumpkin. One custom involves the Urn of Fate, in which friends draw names two at a time from an urn, and pair off for the year. Children set out shoes filled with hay for the Kings' tired camels on Three Kings Day, January 6. Nearly every Spanish house has a manger scene and burning candles above the doorways. Turrón almond candy is a favorite holiday sweet.

## ITALY

Italians set candles in their windows and set up Nativity scenes. In Rome a cannon is fired on Christmas Eve to hail the arrival of the holiday season, after which a sumptuous meal ends a twenty-four-hour fast. Christmas foods include a bread studded with dried fruits, called panettone; dried cod and squid; melons; cappelletti, a pyramid of noodle dough filled with meat, eggs, and spices; and after-dinner nougat candy. Italian children receive their gifts on Three Kings Day.

## GERMANY

The Christmas season runs throughout Advent (a period spanning the four Sundays before Christmas, ending on Christmas Day). An evergreen Advent wreath with four purple candles and one larger white one is displayed, with one candle lit every Sunday and the white one on Christmas Day. Advent calendars with small window openings for each day originated in Germany and are still very popular. Christmas trees, also a German-originated tradition, are elaborately decorated with hand-blown glass balls and bells. In some towns gun or cannon fire sounds on Christmas Day as part of a Christmas tradition that goes back to the legend that a loud sound would awake the woodland spirits. Popular treats are gingerbread men and marzipan, a candy of sugar and almond paste formed into a variety of pretty shapes.

## FINLAND

The Christmas tree is traditionally set out on Christmas Eve and decorated with fruit, candy, paper flags, cotton, tinsel, and lit candles. Families traditionally take a Christmas Eve steam bath before sitting down to a dinner of boiled codfish, potatoes and cream sauce, roast suckling pig or fresh ham, barley porridge, and almonds. Stockings are not hung, but Santa comes in person with costumed elves to pass out presents to the children on Christmas Eve.

9

## MEXICO

Mexicans traditionally enact a nine-day procession symbolic of Mary and Joseph's search for a room in Bethlehem. The travelers are denied shelter until the ninth day, when they discover a representation of the Nativity scene with the Holy Family. Afterward, the participants throw a piñata party. Children poke at a suspended piñata, a decoratively shaped, colorful clay jar, until it breaks, spilling out candy and small toys.

## FRANCE

Instead of a tree, most French homes display a Nativity manger scene, or crèche, sometimes made of clay. A traditional Christmas cake, a bûche de Noël, or "Christmas log," is prepared in the shape of a log. In Provence, French people dressed as shepherds form a procession around the church, which includes a ram-drawn cart holding a newborn lamb. Traditional regional foods include buckwheat cakes and sour cream in Brittany, turkey and chestnuts in Burgundy, and oysters in Paris. French children set out shoes by the fireside, awaiting a visit from Father Christmas. Grown-ups often exchange their Christmas gifts on New Year's Day.

## CANADA

Canadians of English ancestry feast on roast goose or beef and plum pudding, and they decorate with wintergreen and cranberry sprigs. French-speakers in Quebec province open

their presents after midnight mass on Christmas Eve, followed by an elaborate meal of meat pie, turkey, and goose, with fruitcake or bûche de Noël for dessert. The Métis, descendants of French-Indian marriages, hold two weeks of festivities, including gun-firing and feasts of buffalo, moose, and berries, along with fiddle-playing and sleigh rides.

## PHILIPPINES

The holiday festivities run from December 16 to January 6, with masses, pageants, and festivals with carolers and lively brass bands. Lanterns and strings of colored lights illuminate towns and homes. On Christmas Eve local people dress as the Holy Couple and wander through town in search of rooms. Other townspeople follow, and before midnight they all are welcomed at the church, which features a Nativity scene with live animals and children dressed as angels.

## GREECE

The main holiday in Greece is Easter. Christmas trees are uncommon in Greece and gifts are usually exchanged on January 1, Saint Basil's Day, a day that honors one of the four fathers of the Orthodox church. On Christmas morning children sing songs in front of neighboring houses in exchange for dried figs and sweets. These songs are known as *kalanda*. Traditional Christmas foods include pork and Christ bread, a sweet bread fashioned into different shapes.

# December

*December* comes from the Latin word *decem*, meaning "ten." The meaning of the ending *ber*, which occurs in the names of the last four months of the year, is not known.

Under the old Roman calendar, December was the tenth month in a year that began with March and ended with December. When Roman king Numa Pompilius (reigned 715–673 B.C.) added January and February, December was no longer the tenth month, but the name stuck. The Saxons, Germanic people who conquered England, called December *winter monath*, "winter month" and later, after Christianity took hold, *heligh monath*, "holy month."

December is a month of gay Yuletide celebration, but it's also a time of long, dark, and dreary days. This passage from English poet and dramatist William Shakespeare's (1564–1616) *Cymbeline* (act 3, scene 3, lines 36–37) compares the gloomy month to getting old: "What should we speak of/ When we are old as you? when we shall hear/The rain and wind beat dark December."

As we read earlier, Julius I, head of the Western church, set the date for observing Christmas around A.D. 350. However,

Christians in the Eastern church, notably the Eastern Orthodox and the Ukrainian Catholic church, observed Christmas on January 6, a tradition they still maintain. This was because these Christians followed the Julian calendar, established in 46 B.C. by Julius Caesar (100–44 B.C.), not the modern Gregorian calendar, which eliminated what now equals thirteen days, set in 1582 by Pope Gregory XIII (1502–1585).

 **Do You Know**

Although Jesus Christ's date of birth is traditionally accepted as December 25, A.D. 1, some scientists and historians dispute both the month and the year. These experts point out that in the Holy Land, December 25 occurs during the rainy season, pretty nasty weather for shepherds to be tending flocks of sheep. One theory is that Christ was born instead during May, a time when sheep have their lambs. Further, some astronomers believe Christ was born in 6 B.C., not A.D. 1. This conclusion is based on a recent experiment conducted at the Hayden Planetarium in New York City. In recreating the heavens from 6 B.C., it was found that the three planets Mars, Jupiter, and Saturn were close together in a triangular arrangement. Astronomers believe the bright beacon that resulted from these closely aligned planets may have been the biblical Star of Bethlehem that guided people to the Christ child.

# Winter

To understand the word history of *winter*, let's go back to one of the Indo-European languages, those spoken in most of Europe and areas colonized by Europeans. The Indo-European root of *winter* is a form of *wed*, which meant "to be wet, or related to water." The root evolved into Old High German *wintar*, "winter," and Old English *winter*.

The fourth season of the year, winter officially runs from around December 22 to March 20, or from the winter solstice to the vernal equinox. English poet Percy Bysshe Shelley (1792–1822) expressed the frustration many of us share about winter's bleakness in these well-known lines from his poem "Ode to the West Wind": "The trumpet of a prophecy! O, Wind,/If Winter comes, can Spring be far behind?"

Poets and writers sometimes use winter as a figure of speech to suggest old age, as in Shakespeare's comedy *As You Like It* (act 2, scene 3, lines 52–53): "Therefore my age is as a lusty winter,/Frosty, but kindly."

# Do You Know

The word *solstice* comes from two Latin words, *sol*, "sun," and *sistere*, "to stand still." At the time of the winter solstice the midday sun appears low on the horizon. As a result, less direct sunlight reaches the northern hemisphere, which means that there are fewer daylight hours than at any other time of the year.

During the winter solstice, ancient peoples made a symbolic round cracker called a *bretzel*, or *pretzel*, from the Latin *pretiole*, which means "little gift." The pretzel originally had a cross in its center, representing the four seasons. This cross gradually evolved to the pretzel's familiar twist.

# Holiday

*Holiday* arrived in our language from the Old English word *haligdaeg*, from *halig*, "holy," and *doeg*, "day." The two words were combined and written as *halliday*, or "holy day," until the sixteenth century.

In its original meaning, *haligdaeg* referred to a religious day on the church calendar, which is what the first English printer, William Caxton (1422–1491), meant in this line from his translation of the medieval fable "Reynard the Fox": "Go to church, fast and keep your hallidays." In the sixteenth century the meaning of holiday expanded to include any day devoted to recreation and not work. Holly took her holiday vacation from work over the Christmas holidays.

If someone "speaks holiday," they are not using everyday, common words. Shakespeare used this phrase to describe the foolish Sir John Falstaff in his comedy *The Merry Wives of Windsor* (act 3, scene 2, lines 71–73): "He capers, he dances, he has eyes of youth, he writes verses, he speaks holiday, he smells April and May."

# 📜 Do You Know

Did anyone ever criticize you for abbreviating the Christmas holiday to *Xmas*? X is the Greek symbol for Christ from the Greek letter *chi*, written X. Therefore, you are not being disrespectful in writing Xmas.

December 26 in Great Britain is known as Boxing Day, a day unrelated to fighters and knockouts. In the Middle Ages alms boxes were placed in churches at Christmas to collect donations for the poor. Because the boxes were opened on December 26 and their contents distributed to the needy, the day became known as Boxing Day. In nineteenth-century England, servants went to their employers' homes at the holidays hoping to receive money in the boxes they carried. Nowadays in Great Britain, public service people, such as mail carriers and door attendants, still receive gifts on Boxing Day.

# Season

The development of the word *season* has been traced back to the Middle English word *seson* and the French *saison*, both meaning "time of year," from the Latin *serere*, "to sow."

From the biblical book of Ecclesiastes (3:1), we read that

everything has its particular season, or time: "To every thing there is a season, and a time to every purpose under the heaven:/ A time to be born, and a time to die; a time to plant,/ and a time to pluck up that which is planted."

Season is often associated with planting and growing. But English poet John Gay (1685–1732) had a different kind of season in mind when he wrote his satirical ballad opera *The Beggar's Opera*: "Youth's the season made for joys,/Love is then our duty." At the holiday season, Nick only eats food in season.

For many people the holiday season means the Twelve Days of Christmas, extending from December 25 to January 6, also known as Twelfth Night. On the Christian church calendar, January 6 is called Epiphany or Three Kings Day. Epiphany refers to the visit of the three wise men to the infant Jesus, the Adoration of the Magi.

Twelve-day celebrations are not without historic precedents. Early Norsemen in northern Europe held a twelve-day pagan feast to coincide with the dark days of the winter solstice. Amid all the carousing, the Scandinavians burned logs to ward off evil spirits and provide light and warmth.

Over the years Twelfth Night became a good excuse to throw any end-of-the-season holiday bash. In France, on this occasion, merrymakers served a cake with a bean baked inside. Whoever found the bean was toasted as the king or queen of the festivities and was entitled to choose a partner. The most lavish Twelfth Night parties in history were those hosted by French king Louis XIV (1638–1715) at his palace in Versailles.

A favorite song at Christmas is the traditional English carol "The Twelve Days of Christmas." It starts: "On the first day of Christmas my true love gave to me a partridge in a pear tree." Subsequent gifts on days two through twelve included: two turtledoves, three French hens, four colly birds, five gold rings, six geese a-laying, seven swans a-swimming, eight maids a-milking, nine drummers drumming, ten pipers piping, eleven ladies dancing, and twelve lords a-leaping.

## Do You Know

What's a colly bird? *Colly*, a word no longer in common usage, comes from an Old English word *col*, which means "coal." If something was colly, it was darkened with black soot or just plain grimy, so colly birds are simply black birds. When the song is sung today, the lyric is usually changed to "calling birds."

Let's DECK the Halls with
MISTLETOE, HOLLY and IVY,
CANDLES, WREATHS, and
POINSETTIAS, then Decorate the
EVERGREEN TREE with TINSEL
and ORNAMENTS.

# Deck

The root of the word *deck* first turned up in the sixteenth century in the Middle Dutch word *deken*, "to cover." Four hundred years ago people decked both roofs and floors of buildings. In 1599 deck appeared in English as a way of describing the flooring, or platform, on a ship.

Deck also came to mean "to clothe in especially beautiful or ornamental attire," as English novelist Daniel Defoe (1660–1731) wrote in this line from his pamphlet *The Complete English Tradesman*: "Decked out with long wigs and swords."

During the holidays many people and businesses deck their homes and shops with greenery and ornaments. This custom goes back to ancient times when those who worshiped pagan gods decked their dwellings with evergreens. In displaying the greens, these people were paying tribute to gods and spirits who were believed to live in the woods.

The verb "to deck" means to knock someone on the floor with a blow. Ahab, all decked out in his best suit, was taking a turn around the deck when a sailor decked the first mate.

# Mistletoe

The word *mistletoe* is derived from the Old English words *mistel*, "mistletoe," and *tan*, "twig." In German, *mist* means "dung," which may explain the legend that mistletoe's name arose from a belief that its seeds sprouted in bird droppings. A European shrub, mistletoe grows on trees, especially oaks and apples.

In Britain, beginning in the second century B.C., ancient Celtic priests and sorcerers called Druids collected mistletoe to burn as a sacrifice to the gods. So revered was mistletoe that the Druids used a golden sickle to remove sprigs from a sacred oak tree and caught them in a white cloth. The Druids hung mistletoe as a way of guaranteeing good fortune, welcoming people, and urging enemies to bury grudges. And hosts expected their guests to their home to embrace under the mistletoe.

The origin of actually kissing under the mistletoe bough is up for grabs. It may go back to Roman times when enemies meeting under mistletoe reconciled. Or the custom may go back to Frigga, the Norse goddess of love. Frigga and her husband, Odin, had a son Balder, the god of light. In one legend Frigga protected Balder from being harmed by everything, but she forgot to include the mistletoe. Loki, the god of evil, convinced his blind brother to sharpen a sprig of mistletoe and throw it at Balder. It pierced Balder's heart and killed him. Frigga's tears are represented by mistletoe's white berries. When Balder was brought back to life, Frigga was so happy she kissed anyone who walked under the mistletoe.

The Romans decorated their houses with mistletoe boughs during their pagan festivals. Because of the plant's heathen connection, the Christian church banned mistletoe from the church. Herbalist monks called mistletoe *Lignum Sanctae Crucis*, or "the wood of the sacred cross." This refers to the cross of Calvary, on which Jesus Christ was crucified. Mistletoe's dark association is reflected by captured Queen Tamora in Shakespeare's tragedy *Titus Andronicus* (act 2, scene 3, lines 94–95): "The trees, though summer, yet forlorn and lean,/ O'ercome with moss and baleful mistletoe."

Mistletoe also has a long history of medicinal use. The Druids used it in preparations as a cure for many different ailments. People living in France and Sweden wore mistletoe charms to ward off illness. Although parts of the mistletoe plant are poisonous, modern medical research has shown that mistletoe is helpful in treating nerve disorders.

# Holly and Ivy

The source of the word *holly*, a shiny evergreen that's a favorite at Christmas, is the Old English word *holen*, "holly," which in Middle English became *holin*, then *holly*.

Because holly remained green year-round, the ancient Druids considered it a symbol of eternal life and wore sprigs of holly in their hair when they collected the sacred mistletoe. Similarly, the Romans believed that any plant that could survive winter would add strength to their dwellings. They exchanged wreaths of holly at Saturnalia and used it liberally throughout their homes as a winter decoration.

Despite this pagan background, the early Christian church adopted holly as a Christmas symbol. To them holly's pointed green leaves represented the thorns in Christ's crown and its red berries symbolized Christ's blood. In the sixth century a German bishop forbade holly in church because of its heathen association. But by the 1600s the ban on holly was dropped.

Since the midnineteenth century the English have decorated their homes at the holidays with holly. English poet Alfred, Lord Tennyson (1809–1892) wrote painfully about the Christmas after the death of a dear friend, in his elegaic poem

*In Memoriam*: "With trembling fingers did we weave/The holly round the Christmas hearth."

Another seasonal evergreen is ivy. Ivy climbed aboard the English language from the Old English word *ifig* and the Old High German *ebah*, both meaning "ivy."

Like holly, ivy suggested eternal life to the ancients. Sacred to both the Greeks and the Romans, ivy was worn in a crown by the Roman god of wine, Bacchus. The Greeks honored their poets with crowns of ivy.

Although ivy has no special holiday significance in the United States, it's a popular holiday evergreen in England. The two are teamed up in the favorite English Christmas carol "The Holly and the Ivy." A clinging plant, ivy often climbs up walls, adding a decorative covering to old buildings and ruins in England. English poet Thomas Gray (1716–1771) wrote about one ivy-covered structure in his well-known poem *Elegy Written in a Country Churchyard*: "Save that from yonder ivy-mantled tower/The moping owl does to the moon complain."

## Do You Know

# Candle

The Latin verb *candere*, "to shine," gave rise to the Old English *candel*, "candle," and, finally, to our word *candle*. Historically, candles have been linked to the church. In the Greek and Roman churches, wax candles were used because people believed bees came from paradise.

Have you ever heard the phrase "bell, book, and candle"? It was the title of an eerie 1950s movie starring James Stewart. Collectively bell, book, and candle refer to the items used in a Catholic mass. Beginning around 1300, members of the church hierarchy uttered this phrase when they excommunicated someone: "*Doe* (do) *to* the book, quench the candle, ring the bell!" The shortened phrase "bell, book, and candle" conveyed this threat of excommunication some five centuries later in Scottish novelist Sir Walter Scott's (1771–1832) book *The Fair Maid of Perth*: "Hold thy hand, on pain of bell, book, and candle."

Candle is a favorite word of poets for signifying the light of life. Probably the most famous use of this metaphor is in Shakespeare's *Macbeth* (act 5, scene 3, lines 12–16): "Tomorrow, and tomorrow, and tomorrow,/Creeps in this petty pace from day to day,/To the last syllable of recorded time;/And all our yesterdays have lighted fools/The way to dusty death. Out, out brief candle!"

Other popular phrases that contain the word candle include "to hold a candle to," which literally means to help someone in a lower-ranking position by holding a light for them to make their work easier. Today the phrase applies to anyone or anything that falls short, as in English poet John Byrom's (1692–1763) lines, "Others aver that he to Handel/Is scarcely fit to hold a candle." If, on the other hand, you are found guilty of "burning the candle at both ends," you're overdoing things.

To ancient peoples light symbolized life. The Romans tied candles to trees during their December festival of Saturnalia as a way of giving thanks for the sun's return to earth and longer days. Nature-worshiping Celtic priests called Druids lit candles in tribute to Balder, the god of light. German religious reformer Martin Luther (1483–1546) is credited with putting the first candles on Christmas trees.

## Do You Know

Many Christian churches have candlelight services on Christmas Eve. Candles also play a very important role in the eight-day Jewish holiday called Hanukkah, or the Feast of Lights, which takes place in December. In 165 B.C., the Hebrews under Judas Maccabaeus recaptured the Temple of Jerusalem from the Syrians, who had desecrated it. To commemorate their victory of recovered freedom, the Hebrews relit the sacred temple lamps with enough oil to burn for one day. But the lamps burned for eight. In remembering this victory at Hanukkah, Jewish people light one candle a day in a menorah, a candelabra with eight arms, until all eight are burning.

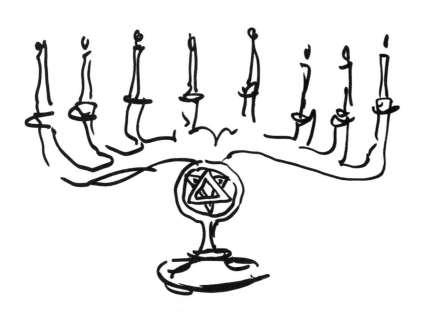

# Wreath

The word *wreath* unfolded in English from the Old English *writhan*, "to twist." In its original meaning, wreath referred to anything that was twisted, especially a circular band of flowers on the heads of noblemen and champions.

In his poem "Song: To Celia," Ben Jonson (1572–1637) writes about offering a rosy wreath. The poem, which has been put to music, contains a beginning you might recognize: ".Drink to me only with thine eyes,/And I will pledge with mine;/Or leave a kiss but in the cup,/And I'll not look for wine. . . . I sent thee late a rosy wreath,/Not so much honouring thee,/as giving it a hope that there/It could not wither'd be."

The four Sundays before Christmas are called Advent Sundays in many Christian churches. The emphasis during Advent, from the Latin *adventus*, "arrival," is on anticipating the arrival of Christmas. Some people in England, Germany, and the United States celebrate the Advent season by displaying an Advent wreath. The evergreen wreath is set with four colored candles to be lit on each Sunday before Christmas, and a larger, usually white one for Christmas Day.

# Poinsettia

The poinsettia plant, which is native to Mexico, has a very small cluster of yellow flowers surrounded by large red, pink, or white leaves. Many people mistake these showy leaves for the flower petals themselves.

The Mexicans call the poinsettia *Flor de la Noche Buena*, "flower of the blessed night," because the starlike shape of the poinsettia reminded them of the Star of Bethlehem.

According to popular belief, Franciscan monks in Mexico first included poinsettias in their Christmas celebrations during the seventeenth century. In another Mexican legend, a young woman too poor to take a gift to place before a statue of the Virgin Mary picked wildflowers along the way. When she placed the flowers in front of the statue, they turned into poinsettia blooms.

President Martin Van Buren's (1782–1862) secretary of war and first minister to Mexico, Dr. Joel Roberts Poinsett (1779–1851), introduced the poinsettia to the United States in 1828. Named in honor of Dr. Poinsett, poinsettias have been in demand at Christmas in this country ever since his death in 1851.

In many cases, plants get their popular names from the person, sometimes a botanist, who first identifies or introduces them. For example, the begonia is named after Michel Bégon, French governor of Santo Domingo in the early eighteenth century, fuchsia after sixteenth-century German botanist Leonhard Fuchs, and gardenia for Alexander Garden, a late-eighteenth-century Scottish naturalist.

# Evergreen Tree

From two Old English words, *aefre*, "always," and *growan*, "to grow," comes our word *evergreen*. Something that is always, or ever, growing is said to be evergreen. The word *tree* has its roots in the Old Norse word *tre*, "tree."

According to one story, the origins of Christmas trees date back to the eighth century in Germany. Then, a Christian monk cut down an oak in front of a group of horrified Celtic Druids, who believed the oak tree sacred. The giant tree crushed everything in its path except for one small evergreen fir tree. The monk considered the tree's survival a miracle and declared the fir the tree of Christ. After that, Christians in Germany planted evergreens at Christmas but they remained undecorated.

A closer relative of the decorated Christmas tree goes back to the fourteenth century. Since few people could read at that time, the church staged mystery plays dramatizing scripture passages. In medieval Germany, during Advent, the story of Adam and Eve was enacted. The lone prop in the play was an evergreen fir tree hung with apples, the Paradise Tree.

By the sixteenth century Germans were decorating fir trees in their homes and churches. People along the upper Rhine River trimmed firs with paper flowers, cookies, fruit, and nuts. In 1539 Strasbourg's Cathedral of Notre-Dame had its first Christmas tree displayed. Nearly a century later a nameless visitor to Strasbourg during the Christmas of 1605 wrote: "For Christmas they have fir-trees in their rooms, all decorated with paper roses, apples, sugar, gold and wafers."

The German custom of trimming evergreens grew slowly in England. In Mrs. Papendick's *Journals* from 1789 she reports: "This Christmas Mr. Papendick proposed an illuminated tree according to the German fashion." The tradition became fashionable after the marriage of Queen Victoria (1819–1901) to German Prince Albert (1819–1861). In 1841 the royal couple set up a decorated Christmas tree in Windsor Castle.

When German immigrants settled in eastern Pennsylvania in the early nineteenth century, they brought with them their custom of decorating trees. From a book titled *Christmas in Pennsylvania*, we know that Christmas trees in the 1820s were decked with homemade and edible decorations—fancy-cut gingerbread; apples; pretzels; flannel rosettes; baskets of nuts; small gifts like handkerchiefs, collars, dolls, and toy wagons and soldiers; and always wax candles.

## Do You Know

Why do many people mount a star atop Christmas trees? From ancient times countless myths have surrounded the stars. Babylonians drew three star symbols to represent the word *god* in their word pictures. The Jewish people adopted the six-pointed Star of David as their symbol. Native Americans believe that every star in the heavens has a human ancestor. For many Christians today, the star on the Christmas tree represents the biblical Star of Bethlehem.

In 1991 the Christmas tree in New York City's Rockefeller Center was wrapped in 25,300 lights, strung on five miles of wiring. The tree, at sixty-five feet high and forty-four feet wide, weighed an impressive twelve tons.

# Tinsel

*Tinsel* is one of those words that, in the course of its history, has undergone a complete change of meaning. It comes from the French word *estincelle*, meaning "a sparkle or flash," from the Latin word *scintillare*, "to sparkle." In the early sixteenth century, tinsel was a kind of cloth, usually made of silk or satin, that was woven with strands of gold or silver. This shimmery brocade fabric was worn only by the very wealthy upper classes.

In English poet Andrew Marvell's (1621–1678) poem "The Definition of Love," love's hope is carried aloft on a richly flashing, brilliant wing: "Magnanimous Despair alone/Could show me so divine a thing, Where feeble Hope could ne'er have flown/But vainly flapped its tinsel wing."

In English, the French *estincelle* was shortened to *tinsel*. And with this change came a flip-flop in meaning. Those who could not afford tinsel invented a less costly substitute. Instead of gold and silver, copper, brass, and tin spangles were sewn into cloth to produce a glittery effect.

Nowadays tinsel refers to something that is showy but inexpensive. The commercial tinsel garlands—and the related icicles—sold to ornament Christmas trees are a good example.

# Ornament

The Latin word *ornare*, meaning "to adorn," is the source of the word *ornament*. It's hard to imagine a Christmas without the twinkling lights and colorful decorations that ornament our trees and buildings.

Other ornaments lend grace and beauty without actually being seen. These invisible ornaments refer to a quality or condition, as the one described by Irish-born English statesman Edmund Burke (1729–1797) in his *Reflections on the Revolution in France*: "Nobility is a graceful ornament to the civil order. It is the Corinthian capital of polished society."

Long before Christianity, people ornamented trees. Druid priests tied apples and candles to oak trees in sacred groves, where they performed magic and healing in secret ceremonies. During their midwinter Saturnalia festival, Roman citizens trimmed trees with candles and pretty objects. The Roman poet Virgil (70–19 B.C.) tells us that the Romans also adorned trees to please their god of wine, Bacchus.

We learned earlier that five hundred years ago the Germans decorated the first Christmas trees with simple handmade and edible trimmings. Today most people in the United States trim

their trees with store-bought glass balls, colored lights, tinsel, garlands, and fancy ornaments. But holiday trees in other countries have their own unique look.

Polish people adorn their trees with decorative angels, peacocks, and other birds. Ukrainians place a spiderweb on their trees for good luck, a tradition that goes back to an old legend of a woman too poor to decorate her tree who found a silvery spiderweb in its branches on Christmas morning. In Sweden people decorate with brightly colored wooden ornaments and straw figures, while Japanese Christians trim their trees with small fans and paper lanterns.

## Do You Know

The Puritans considered trimming a tree at Christmas a pagan mockery of a sacred holiday. From 1659 until the mid-1800s, people in Massachusetts were still subject to fines for putting up Christmas ornaments. Not surprisingly, Massachusetts was the last state to legalize the Christmas holiday, in 1856.

We send MERRY GREETINGS of JOY,
SING CAROLS, and
RING JINGLE BELLS
as we go DASHING through the SNOW.

# Merry

To us when someone is merry they are cheerful. Yet the origin of *merry* is the Old English word *myrge*, which means "short." The jump from "short" to "cheerful" is somewhat of a puzzle to word historians. One possible explanation is that a related verb "to shorten" evolved to mean "to shorten time" and, finally, "to cheer." It's a bit of a leap, but time often seems shorter when we're having a merry time.

When we think specifically of merry people, the first that come to mind may be the band of merry men led by the legendary twelfth-century English outlaw Robin Hood. Merry, however, did not refer to the mood of Robin's band. In those days merry people were those who followed an outlaw or a knight. Sir Walter Scott wrote about these adventurers in his long poem *The Lady of the Lake*: "Still at the gallop prick'd the Knight,/His merry-men follow'd as they might."

Beginning with the fourteenth century, good weather was often described as merry. The phrase "the merry month of May" turns up in many writings, as in this poem by English poet Richard Barnfield (1574–1627): "As it fell upon a day/ In the merry month of May."

English-speakers have been wishing one another a merry Christmas for nearly four hundred years. This international roundup of holiday greetings will tell you how to say "Merry Christmas" in twenty-four different languages.

# We Wish You a Merry Christmas

| | |
|---|---|
| AFRIKAANS | Een Plesierige Kerfees |
| ARABIC | Idah Saidan Wa Sanah Jadidah |
| BOHEMIAN | Vesele Vanoce |
| CHINESE | Kung Hsi Hsin Nien bing Chu Shen Tan |
| CROATIAN | Sretan Bozic |
| CZECH | Vesele Vianoce |
| DUTCH | Vrolyk Kerstfeest |
| FINNISH | Houska Joulua |
| FRENCH | Joyeux Noël |
| GAELIC | Nodlaig mhaith chugnat |
| GERMAN | Froehliche Weihnachten |
| GREEK | Kala Christougena |
| HUNGARIAN | Kellemes Karacsonyi unnepeket |
| ITALIAN | Buon Natale |
| NORWEGIAN | God Jul |
| PILIPINO | Maligayang Pasko |
| POLISH | Boze Narodzenie |

| | |
|---|---|
| PORTUGUESE | Boas Festas |
| RUMANIAN | Sarbatori vesele |
| SERBIAN | Hristos se rodi |
| SPANISH | Feliz Navidad |
| SWEDISH | God Jul |
| UKRAINIAN | Srozhdestvom Kristovym |

# Greeting

*Greet*, the root of the word *greeting*, first appeared in Old English as *gretan*, which meant "to weep." In his mournful poem "There'll Never Be Peace," Scottish poet Robert Burns (1759–1796) wrote about the death of seven brave men and of a tearful visit to their graves: "Now I greet round their green beds in the yard." In Scots and some northern English dialects, greet still carries this mournful sense.

Greet's more popular meaning of "welcome" was in use over a thousand years ago. Then people saluted one another with greetings of welcome that had nothing to do with weeping, as in this example from Shakespeare's tragedy *King Lear* (act 5, scene 1, line 54): "We will greet the time."

At Christmastime, people greet the holiday by sending festive greeting cards. Before printed Christmas cards, people sent handwritten holiday messages. The distinction of producing the first holiday card goes to William Egley, who in 1842, at the age of sixteen, etched a card for general use. The card, of which one hundred were printed, is now preserved in the British Museum. Egley's design featured four scenes that show a holiday party, dancers, skating, a Punch-and-Judy show, a cupid, and a court jester. In 1843 a businessman commissioned London illustrator John C. Horsley (1817–1903) to design a Christmas card. One thousand cards were printed.

Shortly after Horsley's private printing, commercial cards became fashionable, first in England, then Germany. Three decades later, in 1875, a lithographer in Boston named Louis Prang printed the first Christmas cards in the United States.

Prang's cards were too expensive for the general public, and he went bankrupt just before the turn of the century. By then inexpensive Christmas postcards imported from Germany had become all the rage, and they remained popular until 1914. By the time World War I ended, in 1918, the greeting card industry in America had been launched. Today Christmas cards are the best-selling commercial greeting in the United States, with over two billion cards sold every year.

# Joy

Joy sprang up from the Old French word *joie*, "a state of utmost delight." Few poets wrote more eloquently about joy than English poet John Keats (1795–1821). A wonderful example is "Ode to a Nightingale," a poem that praises the eternal beauty of the thrush's nocturnal song: "She dwells with Beauty—Beauty that must die;/And Joy, whose hand is ever at his lips/Bidding adieu."

Apart from meaning delight, joy can also refer to a person. In this example from Shakespeare's tragedy *Antony and Cleopatra* (act 1, scene 5, lines 57–59), Antony misses Cleopatra: "He was not merry,/Which seem'd to tell them his remembrance lay/In Egypt with his joy."

In a religious sense, joy is equated with a place of ultimate joy, or heaven, as exemplified in sonnet 14 by English poet John Milton (1608–1674): "Thy works, and alms . . . Followed thee up to joy and bliss for ever."

A favorite Christmas carol is "Joy to the World!" English pastor Isaac Watts (1674–1748) wrote the words to the carol. But the music, which was inspired by German-born composer George Frideric Handel's (1685–1759) famous oratorio *Messiah*, was not composed until nearly a hundred years after Watts's death.

# Sing

From the Old English word *singan*, "to sing," evolved our word *sing*. Nowadays, in most American towns, there are groups of holiday carolers that sing in one location or move from place to place. According to one popular legend, Saint Francis of Assisi (1181–1226) may have led the very first carol sing around a holiday crèche in Greccio, Italy.

Informal phrases that incorporate sing include "to sing for one's supper." In the nursery rhyme "Little Tommy Tucker," Little Tom sings for his supper of white bread and butter. Tom provided entertainment in exchange for food, which is what the phrase means. "To sing like a canary" is criminal slang for someone who tells all they know, usually to the law.

## Do You Know

In 1950 several songs on the best-selling charts were all Christmas melodies: "All I Want for Christmas (Is My Two Front Teeth)," "Silver Bells," "Christmas in Killarney," and "Frosty the Snowman."

# Carol

Our word *carol* comes down from the Greek word *choraulein*, "ring dance," and the Middle English *carollen*, "to sing joyfully." In ancient times carols were not songs but dances.

Both the Greeks and Romans danced carols in a ring accompanied by flute music. The Romans took these dances to England, where they were performed to a singing accompaniment. By the 1400s in England, the meaning of carol changed to include not only the dance but the singing music that accompanied the dance.

In early England a carol was a joyful song, often compared to the happy warbling of birds, as in Scottish poet Thomas Campbell's (1777–1844) poem "Dead Eagle": "The fife-like carol of the lark." It then followed that joyful songs written for Christmas became known as Christmas carols.

Many of the first Christmas carols were composed in Italy but were lost when the Puritans banned their singing in the sixteenth century. As a result, many of the carols we sing today are relatively recent German, English, and American compositions. "Hark, the Herald Angels Sing" was written in 1737, and "Silent Night, Holy Night" in 1818.

This surviving English carol dates back to the early fifteenth
century.

> I saw a sweet, a seemly sight,
> A blissful bird, a blossom bright,
> That morning made and mirth among:
> A maiden mother meek and mild
> In cradle keep a knave child
> That softly slept; she sat and sung:
> Lullay, lulla, balow,
> My bairn, sleep softly now.

NOTE: In its original meaning, *knave* was a male of humble birth, and *bairn* is Scots for
child.

# Ring

From Old English *hringan* and Middle English *ringen*, which both mean "to ring," came the verb *ring*. For centuries the ringing of bells has announced good and bad news.

In some cases, bells were rung when war broke out. "They now ring the bells, but they will soon wring their hands," ironically observed English statesman Sir Robert Walpole (1676–1745) when England and Spain went to war.

Poet Alfred, Lord Tennyson used the image of ringing bells to create this evocative passage from his long poem *In Memoriam*: "Ring out, wild bells, to the wild sky,/The flying cloud, the frosty light."

Pealing church bells, jingling sleigh bells, and, of course, Santa's bell, typically usher in the holiday season. Some trace Santa's bell-ringing to a legend surrounding Saint Nicholas, who always carried a bell when he brought gifts to children in Europe on the evening before his feast day, December 6. Another theory is that Santa's bell was inspired by the sleigh bells in the poem "A Visit from St. Nicholas," better known as "The Night before Christmas," after its famous first line.

# Jingle Bells

*Jingle* is a word that came into the English language based on a sound. For example, if you pour a handful of pennies into a jar, they make a jingling sound. Words that are based on their imitation of a certain related sound are called echoic. Sizzle, munch, and gurgle are other echoic words. Another tongue-twisting term for these words is onomatopoeic, from the Greek words *onoma*, "name," and *poiein*, "to make."

The sound of jingling coins and keys in our pockets is an ordinary one. But at Christmas jingle takes on a special meaning, thanks to the favorite holiday song "Jingle Bells." The jingling bells in the song are fastened to the horse pulling the sleigh across the fields. In this poem from English poet A. E. Housman's (1859–1936) collection *A Shropshire Lad*, the writer remembers the sound of his workhorses jingling as they ploughed: " 'Is my team ploughing,/That I was used to drive/ And hear the harness jingle/When I was man alive?' "

Another kind of jingle is one created by advertising agencies to sell products on television and radio. These catchy verses or songs encourage us to change our hair color or join a new generation of soda drinkers.

# Bell

The root of the word *bell* developed from the Old English word *belle*, "bell." Church bells have pealed on Christmas Eve ever since the sixth century, except for the early seventeenth century when the Puritans suppressed all Christmas celebrations. *In Memoriam* contains another reference to bells, these at Christmas, which remind the poet Tennyson of the loss of his dear friend: "They bring me sorrow touch'd with joy,/The merry merry bells of Yule."

Whenever bells ring to proclaim a death or disaster, they are said to knell, or toll. Perhaps the most famous lines about bells and death were those penned by English poet John Donne (1572–1631) in his poem *Devotions upon Emergent Occasions*, "Meditation XVII": "No man is an Island, entire of it self;/ . . . and therefore never send to know for whom the bell tolls; It tolls for thee." American novelist Ernest Hemingway (1899–1961) titled his novel *For Whom the Bell Tolls* after Donne's poem.

When something "rings a bell" with you, it stirs your memory. Bells at sea remind sailors of the passing of their watch. A ship's bells ring every half hour, beginning with one bell at 12:30 A.M. Eight bells sound at 4:00 A.M., after which the sequence begins again.

# Dashing

*Dashing* may have arrived in English from the Middle English word *daschen*, "to strike." Some word experts believe that, like jingle, dashing may be an echoic, or onomatopoeic, word, since it imitates the sound of something driving violently ahead.

When English journalist Sir William Howard Russell (1820–1907) covered the Crimean War, he witnessed first-hand the charge of foot soldiers with bayonets: "They dashed on towards that thin red line tipped with steel." Another tragic dashing takes place in Shakespeare's play *The Tempest* (act 1, scene 2, lines 6–8): "A brave vessel/Who had, no doubt, some noble creature in her,/Dash'd all to pieces."

Dashing somewhere involves speed and force, so if you make a forceful statement in your dress, you are said to be "dashing." The adjective "dashing" was first used at the end of the eighteenth century. American essayist Washington Irving (1783–1859) made fine use of it in this passage from his book *Tales of a Traveller*: "She had two dashing daughters, who dressed as fine as dragons."

# Snow

Our word *snow* drifted into the language from the Old English word *snaw*, "snow." Snow is composed of crystals of frozen water that cluster together and hit the ground as snowflakes. When they fall, they mask the earth in white, as American poet and essayist Ralph Waldo Emerson (1803–1882) effectively describes in his poem "The Snow-Storm": "Announced by all the trumpets of the sky,/Arrives the snow, and, driving o'er the fields,/Seems nowhere to alight: the whited air/Hides hills and woods, the river, and the heaven,/And veils the farm-house at the garden's end."

You've probably heard someone use the comparison "as white as snow." One biblical reference for this occurs in the Old Testament book of Isaiah (1:18): "Though your sins be as scarlet, they shall be as white as snow." Shakespeare also equates snow with innocence and purity in *Hamlet* (act 3, scene 1, line 141), when Hamlet advises the troubled Ophelia: "Be thou as chaste as ice, as pure as snow."

Snow can also express a period of time. In the following line from American poet Henry Wadsworth Longfellow's (1807–1882) poem "Burial of the Minnisink," the snows are years: "Thirty snows had not yet shed their glory on the warrior's head."

In the United States the verb *snow* is a slang word for trying to deceive someone by smooth talking. American mystery novelist Hillary Waugh (1920–) used it this way in a passage from *Pure Poison*: "Roger'd be alone in a corner with some girl and . . . looked like he was really snowing them."

## Do You Know

Some snowflakes measure up to an inch across. Their shape depends on temperature and humidity, although most snowflakes are six-sided. There is an endless variety to the different types of snowflakes. A study in 1966 divided them into eighty different classes, among them needles, columns, and hollow prisms.

53

*HO HO HO!*
There's *JOLLY* old *SAINT NICK*,
and up above are
*SANTA CLAUS*
and his *REINDEER*.
*BAH! HUMBUG!* snaps Scrooge,
as the *SLEIGH* flies
out of sight.

# Ho Ho Ho!

There is no record of how *ho* developed as a word in the English language. However, historians do know that since the fifteenth century people have been shouting "Ho!" when they want to point out something. Sailors called out "Land ho!" and in Scandinavia, "Ho!" was a shepherd's cry.

In his historical romance *Westward Ho!*, English clergyman Charles Kingsley (1819–1875) wrote: "Thou too shalt forth, and westward ho, beyond thy wildest dreams." Kingsley was actually describing South America, but the words could just have easily applied to American pioneers settling the American West.

One "Ho!" tells people to look, or come on, let's head west. But when someone on horseback yells "Ho!," it's a signal to the horse to stop, while "Heigh-ho!" and "Tallyho!" spur the horse onward. If, however, you want to poke fun at someone, you'll repeat the cry, as Shakespeare did in his comedy *A Midsummer Night's Dream* (act 3, scene 2, line 421): "Ho, ho, ho, coward, why com'st thou not?"

56

# Jolly

*Jolly* came into English from the Old French word *joli*, "gay and festive." In Shakespeare's comedy *As You Like It* (act 2, scene 7, lines 182–183), one of the lord's attendants sings an amusing song pointing out the fickleness of humanity: "Most friendship is feigning, most loving mere folly:/Then heigh-ho! the holly!/This life is most jolly."

In his book *Julian Home*, English clergyman and writer Frederic William Farrar (1831–1903) wrote these famous lines, which are often sung in tribute at celebrations: "For he's a jolly good fellow, which nobody can deny." Jolly in this case means admirable or excellent, not lively and gay.

Jolly takes on special meaning at Christmas as it applies to gay and lively Saint Nick, described as "chubby and plump, a right jolly old elf" in "The Night before Christmas."

## Do You Know

In the *Dictionary of Vulgar Terms*, published in 1785, a Jolly Roger is defined as a "flag hoisted by pirates." But the designer of the pirate standard remains unknown.

# Saint Nick

There's no doubt that the Latin word *sancire*, "to make sacred," forms the basis of the word *saint*, while the proper noun *Nick* is the shortened name for Nicholas. The historical records surrounding a man named Saint Nicholas, who is considered by many to be the ancestor of our modern Santa Claus, are clouded by legend and speculation. Even the dates of his birth and death are disputed.

We do know a man named Nicholas lived in fourth-century Asia Minor, now Turkey. As a young boy the devout Nicholas entered the seminary, and he later became a bishop. During one of the waves of Christian persecution at the hands of the Romans, Nicholas was tortured and jailed. He was eventually freed by Emperor Constantine the Great (reigned 306–337) and made a saint.

Saint Nicholas was a kind, generous man, particularly fond of children. Because of this, the saint became a legendary figure who was said to deliver gifts to children in Europe on the evening before his feast day, Saint Nicholas Day, December 6. The red-and-white-robed saint made his rounds riding a donkey and carrying a crooked staff.

Following one old legend, on the eve of December 6 Dutch children filled their wooden clogs with straw before they went to bed. They put them on the fireplace hearth along with an apple. The straw was a gift for Saint Nicholas's donkey and the apple for his dreaded assistant, Black Piet, who singled out the naughty children. In exchange for the straw and apple, Saint Nicholas left fruit and trinkets in the shoes.

In sixteenth-century Europe the reformation-minded Protestant church outlawed any mention of the gift-bearing saint. But the Dutch kept this tradition of Saint Nicholas as the bearer of gifts alive. In addition, Dutch sailors adopted Nicholas as their patron saint, and when they sailed to the New World in the early seventeenth century, their ship bows bore carved images of Saint Nicholas.

In America hopeful Dutch children continued to fill their clogs with straw. Saint Nicholas, spelled Sint Nikolaas in Dutch, was anglicized to Sinterklaas. After the Dutch lost control of New Amsterdam later that century, the spelling of Sinterklaas was further anglicized to Santa Claus.

## Do You Know

Centuries ago in Germany and Switzerland, a legendary bearded man named Christkindl, "Christ Child," rode a mule packed with Christmas presents. When the German and Swiss immigrated to Pennsylvania in the eighteenth century, Christkindl came, too. In America, Christkindl became Kriss Kringle.

The three gold balls on a pawnbroker's sign go back to a legend surrounding Saint Nicholas. It's said the charitable bishop helped out a poor family by giving dowries for the three daughters. The three gold balls symbolize the bags of gold Saint Nicholas contributed.

# Santa Claus

As we read, Santa Claus was the English spelling of Sint Nikolaas, the Dutch name for Saint Nicholas. But except for the beard, there was little similarity between this Dutch patron saint of children and our modern-day Santa.

The sleigh-driving, chimney-bounding Santa as we know him acquired his beloved characteristics from a poem written in 1822 called "A Visit from St. Nicholas," better known as "The Night before Christmas." Clement Clarke Moore (1779–1863), a New York professor of theology and classical literature, wrote the poem as a bedtime story to read to his children.

Without including the author's name, an enthusiastic friend

of Moore's sent the poem to a local newspaper, and before long, newspapers and magazines across the country printed the anonymous poem. For fear of damaging his academic standing, Professor Moore waited some sixteen years before publicly admitting he wrote the classic poem.

In the poem Saint Nicholas is a chubby elf with "a round little belly." Santa put on weight over a twenty-year period at the hands of American cartoonist Thomas Nast (1840–1902). His often-reproduced 1881 drawing in *Harper's Weekly* magazine depicted Santa as a pipe-smoking, robust fellow, laden with toys. Nast was also responsible for creating legendary details of Santa's life like his North Pole home, his list-checking habit, and his helpful elves.

# The Night before Christmas

'Twas the night before Christmas, when all through the house
Not a creature was stirring, not even a mouse;
The stockings were hung by the chimney with care,
In hopes that St. Nicholas soon would be there;
The children were nestled all snug in their beds,
While visions of sugar-plums danced in their heads;
And Mama in her kerchief, and I in my cap,
Had just settled our brains for a long winter's nap,
When out on the lawn there arose such a clatter,
I sprang from my bed to see what was the matter.
Away to the window I flew like a flash,
Tore open the shutters and threw up the sash.
The moon on the breast of the new-fallen snow
gave the lustre of midday to objects below,
When, what to my wondering eyes should appear,
But a miniature sleigh, and eight tiny reindeer,
With a little old driver, so lively and quick,
I knew in a moment it must be St. Nick.
More rapid than eagles his coursers they came,
And he whistled, and shouted and called them by name:
"Now Dasher! now, Dancer! now, Prancer and Vixen!
On, Comet! on, Cupid! on Donder and Blitzen!
To the top of the porch! to the top of the wall!
Now dash away! dash away! dash away all!"
As dry leaves that before the wild hurricane fly,
When they meet with an obstacle, mount to the sky,
So up to the house-top the coursers they flew,

With the sleigh full of toys, and St. Nicholas too.
And then, in a twinkling, I heard on the roof
The prancing and pawing of each little hoof.
As I drew in my head, and was turning around,
Down the chimney St. Nicholas came with a bound.
He was dressed all in fur, from his head to his foot,
And his clothes were all tarnished with ashes and soot;
A bundle of toys he had flung on his back,
And he looked like a peddler just opening his pack.
His eyes—how they twinkled! his dimples how merry!
His cheeks were like roses, his nose like a cherry!
His droll little mouth was drawn up like a bow,
And the beard on his chin was as white as the snow;
The stump of a pipe he held tight in his teeth,
And the smoke it encircled his head like a wreath;
He had a broad face and a little round belly,
That shook when he laughed, like a bowlful of jelly.
He was chubby and plump, a right jolly old elf,
And I laughed when I saw him, in spite of myself;
A wink of his eye and a twist of his head
Soon gave me to know I had nothing to dread.
He spoke not a word, but went straight to his work.
And filled all the stockings; then turned with a jerk,
And laying his finger aside of his nose,
And giving a nod, up the chimney he rose;
He sprang to his sleigh, to his team gave a whistle,
And away they all flew like the down of a thistle.
But I heard him exclaim, ere he drove out of sight,
"Happy Christmas to all and to all a good night."

—CLEMENT CLARKE MOORE

65

# Do You Know

In the United States young children wait for Santa Claus to bring presents. In other countries youngsters hope for gifts from other figures.

In Italy the gift-bringer is called La Befana. La Befana, whose name means epiphany, was an old woman who supposedly refused lodging to the Three Wise Men en route to see Jesus Christ. She changed her mind and ran after them but couldn't find them. According to legend, La Befana is still looking for the Christ Child.

The Russian bringer of goodies is Baboushka. According to the story, Baboushka gave wrong directions to the Three Wise Men and like La Befana regretted her action and is still searching for Jesus Christ.

In Spain, Mexico, Puerto Rico, the Philippines, Argentina, and Brazil, children expect gifts from the Three Wise Men.

Children in Poland believe their gifts come from the stars.

In Hungary the angels are said to bring holiday presents.

Driving a sled pulled by goats, a gnome called Jultomten delivers gifts in Sweden.

In Norway the children wait for Jule-nissen. Dressed in red with long white whiskers, Jule-nissen lives all year in a manger in the stable but is visible only at Christmas.

Near Evansville, Indiana, is a small town called Santa Claus. There are conflicting stories as to how it acquired this unusual name. The most amusing has a costumed Santa Claus walking into a meeting in 1882 on Christmas Eve when town names were being considered. Are there any towns in your state with holiday names?

# Reindeer

In "The Night before Christmas," we're told that Saint Nick's miniature sleigh is whisked through the skies by eight tiny reindeer. The word *reindeer* arrived in English from the Old Norse *hreinn*. In English *hreinn* changed to *rein* and hooked up with *dyr*, "deer," to form *reindeer*.

Before the nineteenth century Santa's predecessor, Saint Nicholas, had to deliver his gifts without the benefit of a reindeer-drawn sleigh. Depending on the legend, the humble saint rode a wagon, a donkey, or horse, or walked on foot. As more and more Americans read and treasured "The Night before Christmas," Santa's reindeer were adopted into Christmas lore.

The jolly man's sleigh was pulled by Dasher, Dancer, Prancer, Vixen, Comet, Cupid, Donder, and Blitzen. There's no mention of Rudolph. Where did Santa's ninth reindeer come from? Rudolph became the most famous reindeer of all in 1939. That year Robert L. May, an advertising copywriter for Montgomery Ward in Chicago, wrote a little ditty about Rudolph and his beacon-like nose for the store Santa Claus to distribute. Two million copies of "Rudolph the Red-Nosed Reindeer" were printed—and a legend was born.

Eight years later Johnny Marks put the Rudolph poem to music, and cowboy-singer Gene Autry recorded it in 1949. "Rudolph the Red-Nosed Reindeer" is second only to "White Christmas" as the top-selling single in music history.

# Bah! Humbug!

Like the exclamation ho!, *bah!* is almost always followed by an exclamation point. Bah most likely came into English from the modern French word bah!, an exclamation of scorn. In his poem *Beppo, A Venetian Story*, English poet Lord Byron (1788–1824) wrote, "Dreading the deep damnation of his 'bah!' "

*Humbug*, a slang word first recorded around 1750, means trick, sham, or just plain nonsense. According to a 1751 English publication called *The Student*, *humbug* was originally part of the vocabulary of ruffians but was, surprisingly, adopted by people of class.

Such a refined person was British statesman Lord Randolph Churchill (1849–1895), father of Prime Minister Winston Churchill (1874–1965), who in July of 1884 called Parliament "a gigantic humbug."

Bah! Humbug!, one of the most well-known literary exclamations, was uttered by Ebenezer Scrooge, a character in Charles Dickens's (1812–1870) classic Christmas tale, *A Christmas Carol*. Scrooge, a miserly, mean-spirited man despised by nearly everyone, is described by Dickens as someone who "carried his own low temperature always about . . . and didn't thaw it one degree at Christmas."

So when Scrooge's cheerful nephew wishes him "A merry Christmas, uncle! God save you!" the skinflint replies, "Bah! Humbug!" This is Scrooge's way of saying phooey—Christmas is a fraud. But Scrooge changes his tune after a series of disturbing visions showing Christmases past, present, and future. In a flurry of loving generosity, Scrooge makes amends and showers gifts on everyone, including his devoted, underpaid employee Bob Cratchit and Bob's crippled son, Tiny Tim.

# Sleigh

It was the Dutch bringer of gifts, Saint Nicholas, who in Clement Moore's poem, "The Night before Christmas," drove his sleigh full of toys over the rooftops on Christmas Eve. The Dutch language is also the source of the word *sleigh*, developing from the Dutch *slee*, meaning "sled." *Sled* came from the Old English word *slidan*, "to slide."

Long before the wheel was invented, people used sleds to slide or drag heavy items over the ground. Later, when runners and harnessed animals were added, these sleds became known as sleighs. Like sleds, sleighs were widely used in carting goods, especially in the northeastern United States. American poet

Timothy Dwight (1752–1817) confirmed the sleigh's importance in the late eighteenth century in his book *Travels in New England and New York* when he wrote: "The produce of these tracts is conveyed to market chiefly in sleighs."

Many ski resorts in the United States offer sleigh rides in the winter. If you're lucky enough to take one of these rides, chances are the sleigh will be pulled by horses. If, however, you venture above the Arctic Circle to Lapland, you'll be able to go for a Santa-style sleigh ride with reindeer pulling the sleigh and plenty of blankets and hot drink to keep you warm.

Let's decorate the YULETIDE GIFTS
with RED AND GREEN RIBBON
and fill the STOCKINGS
with CANDY CANES,
TOYS, and NUTCRACKERS.

# Yuletide

The history of the word *Yule* is not clear. Some word historians trace the word back to the Old English word *hiul*, which meant "wheel." Another theory is that it evolved from the Old English word *geol*, "yule," and coupled with *tid*, "time," became *Yuletide*. In Old Norse *jol* was a pagan feast that lasted twelve days.

Although to us Yuletide means the Christmas holiday season, the background surrounding the word Yule has no connection to our religious holiday. It's believed Yule was a time when primitive peoples celebrated the return of the sun, or the winter solstice. Reassured that the time of dark days had past, people lit huge bonfires.

In Scandinavia, the ceremony of gathering the log for these Yule fires became very significant. The Scandinavians selected large logs from either an apple or oak tree and used an unburned piece of log from the previous year to light the new log.

The ancient pagan traditions surrounding the gathering and lighting of the Yule log went on to become firmly rooted in the celebration of Christmas, especially in medieval England. There, as Christmas approached, a tree was cut, and the Yule log was marked and then left in the forest. Later, people went out to find the log and drag it back from the woods. One half was set into the fireplace, and the other was saved to use as kindling wood.

Long considered a symbol of good luck, the Yule log is associated with several superstitions. Yule ashes were saved to protect houses from lightning. Ashes were also mixed with water and taken internally as a cure for stomach disorders and used externally to apply to infections.

## Do You Know

Today we decorate a Christmas tree instead of gathering and burning a Yule log. But at the Ahwahnee Hotel in Yosemite National Park, in California, a Yule log is lit every year amid a festive ceremony.

# Gift

*Gift* made its way into our language via the Old English verb *giefan*, "to give," and then *gift*, "offering." We've already read about the theory that Christmas may have its roots in the Roman festival of Saturnalia. The giving of gifts was an important part of this midwinter celebration. The Romans exchanged gifts of honey, silver and gold coins, fruit, pastries, and oil lamps. Youngsters typically received small carved clay figurines. The wealthy made generous contributions to the poor, and the poor gave gifts of holly garlands and candles.

Early Christians may have given gifts at Christmas. But if they did, it would have been against the wishes of the church, which considered gift-giving a leftover tradition from pagan times. In spite of church opposition, most Europeans were swapping Yuletide presents by the twelfth century. At that time children were often given three gifts—one that was useful, an entertaining one, and a disciplinary gift.

Material gifts are given to us, but we also have natural gifts of our own. Gabriel, a gifted singer, was asked to present the retirement gift to the choirmaster because he also had the gift of gab.

# ? Do You Know

Did anyone ever tell you to "never look a gift horse in the mouth?" English poet Samuel Butler (1612–1680) may have said it first, in a long poem satirizing the Puritans titled *Hudibras*: "He ne'er consider'd it, as loth/To look a gift-horse in the mouth." You can pretty well fix a horse's age from the state of its teeth. But you shouldn't be so rude as to examine dentures of a horse given to you. In other words, be grateful for the unexpected—and expected—gifts you receive.

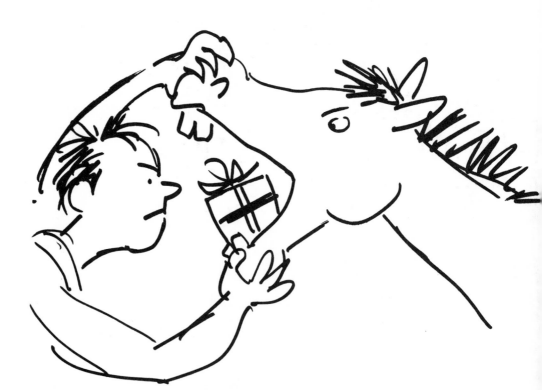

# Red and Green

Why are red and green considered the traditional colors of Christmas? It may have all started with the popularity of red-berried green holly among ancient peoples. There is, however, no history to support this. In the church's view, white, signifying purity and light, is the true color of Christmas.

The word *red* emerged from the Old English word *read*, "red." Over the centuries red, the color of blood, was associated with rebellion and war. In the Catholic Church red stood for honor and charity. For this reason ecclesiastical robes were red, and saints' days on church calendars were marked in red, giving rise to the phrase "a red-letter day," or an important day.

Green filtered down from the Old English word *grene*, related to growan, "to grow." Unlike red, which has been linked with conflict and honor, green's association has always been with hope and youth, especially reflected in a time of budding new growth. In the ballad "Barbara Allen," an anonymous poet writes: "All in the merry month of May,/When green buds they were swellin'."

# Ribbon

*Ribbon* was woven into the English language from the Middle English word *riban* and the Middle French word *ruban*, both meaning "ribbon."

People have been using narrow bands of decorative material to ornament clothing for over four centuries. When Queen Elizabeth I (1533–1603) reigned in England, she chose from some 159 different kinds of ribbons for hair and clothing, including shoes and hats. The poem "My Mother Bids Me Bind My Hair" by English poet Anne Hunter (1742–1821) illustrates the versatility of these fashionable ribbons: "My mother bids me bind my hair/With bands of rosy hue,/Tie up my sleeves with ribbons rare,/And lace my bodice blue."

Ribbon also describes anything that takes the shape of coiled ribbon, such as a road or even moonlight, as English poet Alfred Noyes (1880–1958) evokes in his best-known poem, "The Highwayman": "The road was a ribbon of moonlight

over the purple moor,/And the highwayman came riding—riding . . ./The highwayman came riding, up to the old inn-door."

Before the manufacture of ribbon became big business at the turn of the century, people wrapped their packages in brown paper, and they glued on colorful cutout picture scraps. The late 1800s also saw an explosion of mass-produced items. So instead of exchanging handmade gifts, people bought mass-produced ones. Since a store-bought present lacked the personal touch, shopkeepers encouraged customers to wrap their gifts with colorful paper and ribbons.

Ribbons adorn packages but they are also awarded as prizes to winners of everything from Best Horse to Tastiest Horse-radish at the county fair. Julie lost her red hair ribbon riding Grosgrain over the ribboning cross-country trail but took a blue ribbon at the horse show.

# Stocking

*Stocking* found its way into the English language from the Old High German word *stoc*, "stick," and the verb *stock*, which meant "to cover with a stocking." After all, we do stick our feet into stockings. And when the seventeenth-century Puritans wanted to publicly punish offenders, they secured their feet in wooden stocks.

The association of stockings, or socks, with money and good fortune goes back centuries, to prebank times, when people jammed their savings first into shoes, then into more expandable socks. Even today we talk about people who have socked away a lot of cash, probably in a bank, however, instead of in their argyles.

We can only speculate on how the custom of hanging stockings on the mantle at Christmas got started. In one English legend, Father Christmas dropped some coins while climbing down the chimney and they landed in a stocking hung up to dry. Next morning the unexpected windfall was gleefully discovered by the sock's owner.

A related tale also pairs Saint Nicholas with stocking-filling. When Nicholas gave three penniless daughters their dowries, he threw bags of gold pieces down the house's smoke hole. And, again, some of the coins landed in a wet stocking. In *Diedrich Knickerbocker's History of New York*, Washington Irving's satirical look at the Dutch who settled New York in the early 1600s, the author describes the Dutch custom "of hanging up a stocking in the chimney on Saint Nicholas eve; which stocking is also found in the morning miraculously filled."

Whether it was an English or Dutch tradition, the custom of hanging up a Christmas sock was no doubt bolstered by the well-known line from "The Night before Christmas": "The stockings were hung by the chimney with care."

After spending two days in the stocks for working on Sunday, John pulled up his socks, counted up the money he had socked away, and took stock of his future.

# ❔ Do You Know

Stockings were first worn only by men. There are few references to women wearing them until Queen Elizabeth I's reign. Among the many elaborate Christmas gifts Queen Elizabeth received from her subjects was a pair of silk stockings, perhaps the first to appear in Europe.

# Candy Cane

*Candy* goes back to an Arabic and Persian word *qand*, which means "cane sugar." The chief ingredient in candy is sugar, and refined sugar is produced from the juices of sugar-cane and sugar beets. The word *cane* grew in English from the Greek word *kanna*, from the Arabic word for "reed," *qanah*.

Cane came to mean a stick for walking in 1590. Shaped like a walking stick, the candy cane is the perfect shape to hang on Christmas tree boughs. The source for the striped pattern of the hard candy was no doubt the barber pole, with its alternating red-and-white stripes.

Long before sugar was discovered, the Egyptians made candy by blending honey with figs, dates, nuts, and spices. The first sugar was processed from the juice of sugarcane either in India or Persia during the fourth century A.D. Candy was not manufactured on a large scale until the fourteenth century, when the Venetians turned imported sugar into sweet confections. The mechanization of the nineteenth-century Industrial Revolution paved the way for mass-producing candy. Among the earliest commercial sweets were Tootsie Rolls, in 1896, and Life Savers, in 1913.

# Toy

The story behind the history of the word *toy* is a puzzling one. The word *toye*, meaning "to flirt or trifle with," was in general usage in English by 1300. The phrase "to toy with someone's affection" evolved from this. Then toy mysteriously disappeared from the language until some two hundred years later, when it reappeared with a different meaning.

In 1530 toy was something that had little or no value. These lines spoken by Macbeth in Shakespeare's play *Macbeth* (act 2, scene 3, lines 97–99) illustrate this nicely: "From this instant,/ There's nothing serious in mortality:/All is but toys."

Later in the sixteenth century toy grew to mean a play object. Scottish poet Robert Louis Stevenson (1850–1894) wrote *A Child's Garden of Verses*, expressly for children. Of

the many references to toys, this one describes a thought no doubt shared by many youngsters: "When I am grown to man's estate/I shall be very proud and great,/And tell the other girls and boys/Not to meddle with my toys." If Brian toyed with his food, his favorite toys were locked away.

Before the Civil War most rural children received hand-made Christmas toys. Dolls were stuffed with straw and wore rag dresses. If you lived in a big city and your family could afford it, you might have found an imported mechanical soldier or porcelain doll under the Christmas tree. After the Civil War American factories began turning out mass-produced toys, such as windup boats, dollhouses, and music boxes.

Best-loved Christmas toys at the turn of the century included stuffed teddy bears and electric trains. Although there's been a swing in popularity of Christmas toys, many have sold consistently well for a century, especially trains, sleds, dolls, mechanical toys, and stuffed animals.

# Nutcracker

The two words that make up *nutcracker*, a tool for cracking open nuts, both evolved from Old English words: *hnutu*, "nut," and *cracian*, "cracker."

In the nineteenth century nutcrackers in fanciful shapes were given to both adults and children as gifts, especially at Christmas. In a letter from Doctor Sheridan dated September 15, 1736, contained in English satirist Jonathan Swift's (1667–1745) collected correspondence, we read: "I shall send . . . about six Quarts of nuts to Mrs. Whiteway . . . with a fine pair of Cavan [an Irish county] nut-crackers to save her white teeth."

Ironically, it's the nutcracker under the Christmas tree in German author E. T. A. Hoffmann's (1776–1822) story "The

Nutcracker and the Mouse King" that breaks its teeth, when young Fritz forces huge nuts into its mouth. The story is a fanciful tale of Fritz and his sister, Marie, who becomes devoted to the broken toy. Russian composer Pyotr Ilich Tchaikovsky (1840–1893) wrote the music for *The Nutcracker* ballet. First performed in Saint Petersburg in 1892, the ballet is a perennial holiday favorite here and abroad.

## Do You Know

When British paleontologists Mary and Louis Leakey uncovered a fossil in 1959 in Tanzania, they found it had unusually well-developed teeth. They determined that the specimen, which they nicknamed Nutcracker Man, was the oldest example of a person who made tools from stone.

CHESTNUTS are roasting on the fire,
and there are plenty of COOKIES,
EGGNOG, MINCE PIE, WASSAIL,
and PLUM PUDDING.

# Chestnut

The word *chestnut* appeared in English from the Middle English word *chasteine*, "chestnut tree," and later *chesten*, from the Latin word for chestnut, *castanea*. *Castanea* got its name from the ancient city of Kastanaia, located in what is now Turkey. Roasting chestnuts over an open fire is a favorite winter pastime, especially at Christmas. In 1946 American singer-pianist Nat King Cole first sang about it in "The Christmas Song," with its well-known reference to "chestnuts roasting on an open fire."

The word chestnut is also slang for a story repeated too often. Word historians can't explain its history but believe its use originated in the United States. One explanation relates to an article in a late-nineteenth-century American newspaper. In it someone is telling a stale story about a cork tree, but a listener corrects the teller, saying the tree is: "A chestnut, I should know as well as you, having heard you tell the tale these twenty-seven times."

Another curious phrase is "to pull your chestnuts out of the

fire," or to do dangerous work for someone else. This goes back to an old fable about a monkey that used a cat's paw to fetch dangerously hot chestnuts from a fire.

## Do You Know

Early in this century chestnut trees in this country fell victim to a fungus, similar to Dutch elm disease, that killed all large trees. Chestnuts today come from European trees.

# Cookie

The word *cookie* evolved from the Dutch word *koek*, "cake," into *koekje*, "a small cake, or cookie." In Scotland plain unsweetened buns sold at bakeries are known as cookies. In England cookies are called "biscuits," so if someone there offers you a biscuit with your tea, expect a sweet cookie.

In the United States cookie is an informal term for a good-looking woman, especially in detective fiction and movies. A man is called a cookie only if preceded by an adjective; for example, "he's one smart cookie."

The phrase "that's how the cookie crumbles," meaning that's the way things go, is a recent expression that appeared in this quote about television comedian Milton Berle, in the September 7, 1957, issue of the *Saturday Evening Post*: "From then on, that's the way the cooky crumbled, I enjoyed having good ratings, but I didn't enjoy the viciousness of the railbirds' thrusts at Berle."

People around the world—from Britain to Brazil—enjoy baking cookies at Christmas. We owe a debt to the Germans who immigrated to Pennsylvania for introducing this tradition in the United States. German bakers cut out cookies in many different shapes, including rabbits, stars, and deer, and used the cookies to decorate their Christmas trees.

"Marlowe is one tough cookie who really takes the cake," said Detective F. Newton, brushing cookie crumbs off his tie.

# Eggnog

The word *egg* entered the English language from the Old English word *aeg*, "egg." Although there is no recorded word history for *nog*, we do know that in the early 1600s nog was a small block of wood. By the end of the century, the English drank a strong beer called nog.

In the middle of the nineteenth century, eggnog was created when creative Englishmen took this strong beer and added eggs beaten until foamy. Cider, wine, or hard liquor such as whiskey were often substituted for the beer. This deliciously rich concoction became a special holiday drink.

American novelist Albion Tourgée (1838–1905), who wrote about Reconstruction in the American South, described one of the problems with eggnog in his story "Zouri's Christmas": "Then he tried to drain the glass, but a part of the foamy nog remained in it despite his efforts."

Over the years several phrases and slang uses have developed involving the word egg. To goof in American slang is "to lay an egg." English poet William Cowper (1731–1800) observed, "Remorse, the fatal egg by pleasure laid," in his poem "Report of an Adjudged Case."

If you "put all your eggs in one basket," you're risking everything on the success of one venture. Here English author D. H. Lawrence (1885–1930) gives some romantic advice in his essay "Reflections on the Death of a Porcupine": "It is a pity that we have insisted on putting all our eggs in one basket; calling love the basket, and ourselves the egg."

An egghead is someone whose head is shaped like an egg. In this country an intellectual is sometimes called an egghead. Diplomat Adlai Stevenson (1900–1965), who appealed strongly to intellectuals, ran unsuccessfully against Dwight D. Eisenhower (1890–1969) in the presidential race of 1952. Candidate Stevenson made this humorous remark in the *Daily Telegraph*: "Eggheads of the world, unite, you have nothing to lose but your yolks."

# Mince Pie

*Mince* came into English from the Middle French word *mincer*, "to cut in small pieces," which most likely developed from the Latin word *minutia*, "smallness." Edward Lear (1812–1888) was an English painter who also wrote nonsense verse. One of his poems, "The Pelican Chorus," goes like this: "They dined on mince, and slices of quince,/Which they ate with a runcible spoon [fork with three broad prongs];/And hand in hand, on the edge of the sand,/They danced by the light of the moon."

Mince is a culinary term. Cooks mince onions and vegetables—cut them into small pieces. In a figurative sense, even words can be minced. The familiar expression "mincing words" is usually stated in the negative. People who don't mince words give their opinions plainly and frankly.

A traditional holiday dessert is mince pie, a dessert that originated in England. In 1596 English mince pies were called mutton pies, since they were made from lamb. These early pies were baked in the form of a manger. Bakers today cut up small pieces of beef, hardened animal fat (called suet), and apples, and mix them with sugar, molasses, cider, raisins, citron, fruit juice, and spices.

# Wassail

*Wassail* comes to us from two Old English words, *waes hael*, which meant "good health." In the Middle Ages people toasted their guests by saying *wassail*, or "here's to your good health," after offering them a cup of wine. The reply was *drinkhail*, "let's drink."

The first known use of this phrase goes back to English historian Geoffrey of Monmouth (ca. 1100–1155), in his account of a young Saxon woman named Rowena who offered a bowl of wine to a handsome prince and said, *"waes hael."*

In the fourteenth century this spicy wassail brew consisted of mulled ale, eggs, curdled cream, nutmeg, cloves, and ginger, with floating roasted apples. Wassail ale was served at Old English feasts in a large wooden bowl, although one legend states the Saxons drank ale from their enemies' skulls. During this time young men went from house to house carrying small wassail bowls, singing carols in exchange for food or tokens.

Historians believe it was King Henry VIII of England

(1491–1547) who made wassail a Christmas tradition in the early sixteenth century. During the holidays the characters in Charles Dickens's humorous book *The Pickwick Papers* sat down to: "a mighty bowl of wassail . . . in which the hot apples were hissing and bubbling."

Today in the United States, we go a-wassailing when we sing carols, but most holiday hosts offer eggnog in a punch bowl instead of wassail.

# Twentieth-Century Christmas
# Wassail Punch

6 apples for baking
½ cup apple juice
¼ cup brown sugar
spice mixture: 1 whole nutmeg, 3 whole cloves, 3
    allspice berries, 1 stick cinnamon (broken into pieces)
½ cup water
½ gallon apple cider
2½ cups cranberry or apricot juice

Core apples and peel a narrow strip around top of each. Place in small baking dish. Mix apple juice and brown sugar and bring to a boil in a saucepan. Pour mixture over apples, cover pan with foil, and bake for 30 minutes at 350 degrees.

Drain syrup from apples. Add water to syrup and place mixture in saucepan. Mix spices together and enclose in a bag made from cheesecloth. Tie top with string. Place spice bag in reserved syrup and water mixture and simmer for 15 minutes. Stir in apple cider and cranberry or apricot juice. Heat until mixture is steaming. Remove spice bag, pour punch into a festive holiday bowl, and float the baked apples on top.
  Don't forget to toast *waes hael!*

# Plum Pudding

Plum pudding is made up of the Old English *plume* from Latin *prunum*, "plum," and *pudding* from the Middle English *puddyng*, a word of unknown origin. In the fourteenth century puddings were made by boiling the stomach of an animal, such as a pig or sheep, that had been first stuffed with a mixture of suet, oatmeal, and seasonings.

The English began eating plum puddings in the late seventeenth century as part of their regular meals. They called the puddings "plum" because they were made with dried fruits like raisins, which were called plums. Other pudding ingredients were meat broth, chopped animal tongues, fruit juice, wine, and spices.

In modern times plum pudding usually contains animal fat called suet, instead of broth or tongue. According to an old tradition, cooks are supposed to make a wish when stirring the pudding. Before it's served, some people soak their plum pudding in liquor and then flame it.

Plum pudding may have become a holiday tradition thanks to English King George I (1660–1727). Since he had not tasted plum pudding in his native Germany, he requested one be served at his first English Christmas dinner, in 1714. Plum pudding with hard sauce has been on the Christmas dinner menu at the White House for over a century.

*The White House Cookbook* by Hugo Ziemann and Mrs. F. L. Gillette, published in 1905, tells us what else the president's fifty guests dined on during a typical multicourse Christmas meal:

oysters on the half shell
game soup (rabbit, venison, grouse)
boiled white fish with sauce *maître d'hôtel*
roast goose with applesauce
boiled potatoes
mashed turnips
creamed parsnips
stewed onions
boiled rice
lobster salad
canvasback duck
vanilla ice cream
mince pie
orange jelly
delicate cake (made with egg whites and cornstarch)
salted almonds
confectionery
fruit
water, champagne, and four different wines
coffee

# 🍬 Do You Know

If you were to take a fruitcake poll in this country, those who claim to actually like the dessert would probably be in the minority. Yet fruitcakes are a popular gift during the holidays, and chances are you'll be served at least one piece at a Christmas dinner.

The first fruitcakes were baked in the Middle Ages, when flour was added to fruits and nuts, and the mixture was then baked in a frying pan over an open fire. Later the English came up with their own version, called a prophecy cake, and offered it on January 6. Some of these cakes were decorated with colorful icings and contained coins or thimbles inside. In fruitcake lore, whoever found the coin would be assured wealth in the new year; the thimble promised peace on the home front.

# Timeline

*This chart is meant to give readers a general time frame as well as specific points of reference to topics mentioned in this book.*

---

| | |
|---|---|
| 165 B.C. | Hebrews recapture Temple of Jerusalem from Syrians |
| ca. 50 B.C. | Romans decorate trees to honor Bacchus |
| 0 | Christian era begins |
| A.D. 43 | London founded |
| ca. 300 | Bishop Nicholas becomes a saint |
| ca. 350 | Sugar processed from sugarcane in India or Persia |
| ca. 500 | The German church forbids use of holly as decoration |
| ca. 500 | Dark Ages begin in Europe |
| 800 | Charlemagne crowned first Holy Roman Emperor in Rome |
| ca. 1050 | First German Christmas carol composed |
| ca. 1200 | Saint Francis of Assisi leads the first carol sing in Italy |
| ca. 1300 | Venetians make candy |

| 1530 | Charles V crowned Holy Roman Emperor |
| 1539 | Strasbourg's Cathedral of Notre-Dame displays its first public Christmas tree |
| ca. 1600 | Church's ban on holly dropped in Europe |
| 1642 | Puritans in England under Oliver Cromwell ban Christmas |
| 1659 | Puritans in Massachusetts enact laws against Christmas celebrations |
| 1660 | England's King Charles II revives Christmas |
| 1685 | Composer of the *Messiah*, George Frideric Handel, born |
| 1714 | King George I eats plum pudding |
| 1820s | German immigrants in Pennsylvania decorate holiday trees |
| 1822 | Clement C. Moore writes "A Visit from St. Nicholas" |
| 1828 | Dr. Joel Poinsett introduces poinsettia from Mexico |
| 1837 | German Princess Helen of Mecklenburg introduces Christmas tree to Paris |
| 1841 | Queen Victoria and Prince Albert set up a Christmas tree in Windsor Castle |
| 1842 | William Egley, sixteen, designs the first Christmas card for general use in England |

| | |
|---|---|
| 1843 | John Horsley's Christmas card is privately printed in London |
| | Charles Dickens writes *A Christmas Carol* |
| 1856 | Massachusetts is the last state to legalize Christmas |
| 1875 | Lithographer Louis Prang prints first Christmas card in U.S. |
| 1881 | Cartoonist Thomas Nast illustrates Santa Claus in *Harper's Weekly* |
| 1892 | *The Nutcracker* ballet first performed in Saint Petersburg |
| ca. 1900 | People in U.S. send imported German Christmas postcards |
| 1933 | Rockefeller Center displays first formal Christmas tree |
| 1939 | Poem "Rudolph the Red-Nosed Reindeer" written |
| 1946 | Singer Nat King Cole records "The Christmas Song" |
| 1949 | Cowboy-singer Gene Autry records "Rudolph the Red-Nosed Reindeer" |
| 1950 | "Frosty the Snowman" record makes the top ten |

# Bibliography

ETYMOLOGY

*The Oxford Dictionary of English Etymology.* Oxford: Clarendon Press, 1966.
    The *ne plus ultra* for all word sleuths.
Shipley, Joseph T. *Dictionary of Word Origins.* New York: Philosophical Library, 1945.
    Word histories in capsule form written in a lively anecdotal style.
*Webster's New Collegiate Dictionary.* Springfield, Mass.: G. C. Merriam Company, 1977.
    My own personal dictionary favorite, with an invaluable listing of biographical and geographical names.

CHRISTMAS INFORMATION AND LORE

Brasch, R. *How Did It Begin?* New York: David McKay Company, 1965.
    Traces roots and backgrounds of many familiar customs and traditions. Creatively arranged, with good index.
Cohen, Hennig, and Tristram Potter Coffin, eds. *The Folklore of American Holidays.* Detroit: Gale Research Company, 1987.
Grun, Bernard. *The Timetables of History.* New York: Simon & Schuster, 1975.
    Lists concurrent world events in seven different fields of endeavor.

Hatch, Jane M. *The American Book of Days*. New York: H. W. Wilson Company, 1978.

Rich in historical information.

Hillier, Bevis. *Greetings from Christmas Past*. London: Herbert Press, 1982.

Chockful of insights into English Yuletide traditions.

Lee, Kay, and Marshall Lee, eds. *The Illuminated Book of Days*. New York: G. P. Putnam's Sons, 1979.

A delightful pastiche of facts, illustrated by Kate Greenaway, that will carry you through all the seasons.

Myers, Robert J. *Celebrations: The Complete Book of American Holidays*. Garden City, N.Y.: Doubleday & Company, 1972.

A treasure trove of holiday lore and customs.

Panati, Charles. *Extraordinary Origins of Everyday Things*. New York: Harper & Row, 1987.

A fascinating, painstakingly researched volume that will satisfy your curiosity on a wide range of subjects.

# Suggestions for Additional Reading

Barth, Edna. *Holly, Reindeer, and Colored Lights.* New York: Seabury Press, 1971.

Dalgleish, Alice, ed. *Christmas Stories Old and New.* New York: Charles Scribner's Sons, 1962.

Karas, Sheryl Ann. *Solstice Evergreen.* Boulder Creek, Calif.: Aslan Publishing, 1991.

Krythe, Maymie R. *All About Christmas.* New York: Harper & Brothers, 1954.

Mulherin, Jennifer. *The Little Book of Christmas.* New York: Crescent Books, 1991.

Reeves, James, comp. *The Christmas Book.* New York: E. P. Dutton & Co., 1968.

Robbins, Maria, and Jim Charlton. *A Christmas Companion.* New York: Perigee Books, 1989.

Yolen, Jane. *Hark! A Christmas Sampler.* New York: G. P. Putnam's Sons, 1991.

# Index

115

116